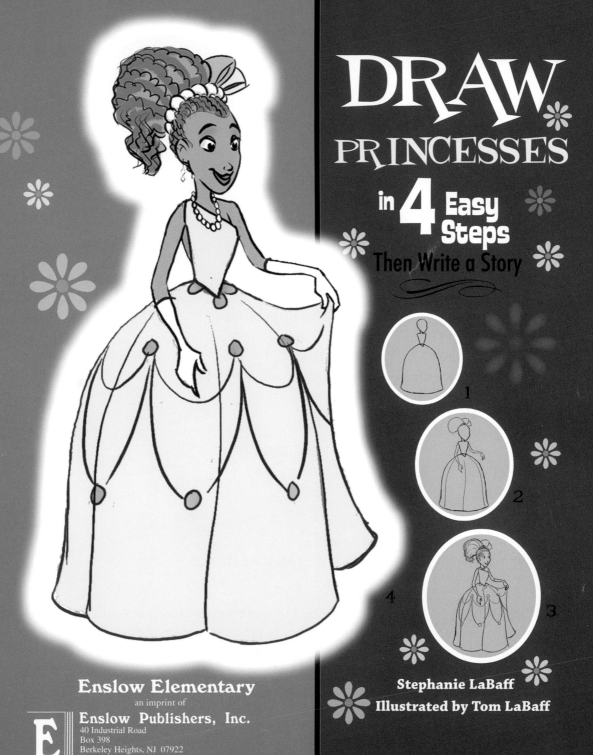

DRAW PRINCESSES

in 4 Easy Steps

Then Write a Story

1

2

4

3

Stephanie LaBaff

Illustrated by Tom LaBaff

Enslow Elementary

an imprint of

Enslow Publishers, Inc.

40 Industrial Road
Box 398
Berkeley Heights, NJ 07922
USA

http://www.enslow.com

Enslow Elementary, an imprint of Enslow Publishers, Inc.
Enslow Elementary® is a registered trademark of Enslow Publishers, Inc.

Library of Congress Cataloging-in-Publication Data
LaBaff, Stephanie.
  Draw princesses in 4 easy steps : then write a story / by Stephanie LaBaff ; illustrated by Tom LaBaff.
      p. cm. — (Drawing in 4 easy steps)
  Includes index.
  Summary: "Learn to draw fairy tale characters and write a story about them, with a story example and story prompts"—Provided by publisher.
  ISBN 978-0-7660-3838-7
  1. Princesses in art—Juvenile literature. 2. Drawing—Technique—Juvenile literature.
  3. Fantasy fiction—Authorship—Juvenile literature. I. LaBaff, Tom. II. Title. III. Title: Draw princesses in four easy steps.
  NC825.P75L33 2012
  743.4'4—dc22
                              2010048149
Paperback ISBN 978-1-4644-0011-7
ePUB ISBN 978-1-4645-0463-1
PDF ISBN 978-1-4646-0463-8

Printed in the United States of America
092011 Lake Book Manufacturing, Inc., Melrose Park, IL
10 9 8 7 6 5 4 3 2 1

To Our Readers: We have done our best to make sure all Internet Addresses in this book were active and appropriate when we went to press. However, the author and the publisher have no control over and assume no liability for the material available on those Internet sites or on other Web sites they may link to. Any comments or suggestions can be sent by e-mail to comments@enslow.com or to the address on the back cover.

♻ Enslow Publishers, Inc., is committed to printing our books on recycled paper. The paper in every book contains 10% to 30% post-consumer waste (PCW). The cover board on the outside of each book contains 100% PCW. Our goal is to do our part to help young people and the environment too!

Contents

Getting Started

Lots of Paper

Pencil sharpener

your IMAGINATION

↑ PenciL

Eraser

Drawing princesses and castles is as easy as 1, 2, 3, 4! Follow the 4 steps for each picture in this book. You will be amazed at what you can draw. After some practice, you will be able to make your own adjustments, too. Change a pose, move an arm, or draw a different dress. There are lots of possibilities!

Follow the 4 Steps

1 Start with big shapes, such as the head and body.

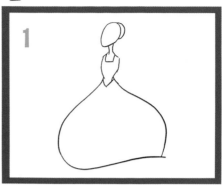

2 Add smaller shapes, such as the arms and hands. In each step, new lines are shown in red.

3 Continue adding new lines. Erase lines as needed.

4 Add final details and color. Your princess will come to life!

Princess Eva

1

2

Erase the dotted lines under her dress.

3

4

Princess Trina

1

2

3

Erase the dotted line at the top of her skirt and under her right arm.

4

Princess Drew

1

2

3

4

Princess Sierra

1

2

3

Erase the dotted lines that show through the bottom of her dress.

4

Princess Stella

1

2

3

Erase the dotted lines that show through her arm and along the horse's face.

4

Prince

1

2

3

Erase the dotted lines under his hair.

Erase the dotted lines underneath his collar.

4

Fairy Godmother

1

2

3

Erase the line across the top of her crown.

4

Woodsman

1

2

3

Erase the dotted lines behind his face, hat, and left arm and hand.

4

Witch

1

2

3

Erase the dotted lines that go across
her arm, through her nose, and
along the edge of her cape.

4

Goose

1

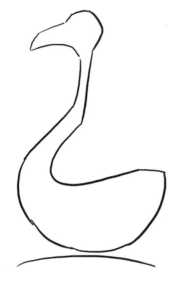

2

3

Erase the dotted lines behind the legs and wing, and along the tail feathers.

4

Mouse

1

2

3

Erase the dotted lines behind the arm and feet.

4

Frogfish

1

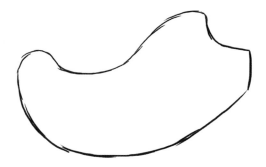

2

3

Erase the dotted lines behind the fins, the mouth, and the throat.

4

Toad

1

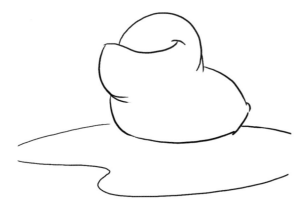

2

Leave part of each pupil white so that it looks shiny.

Erase the dotted lines behind the eyes and legs.

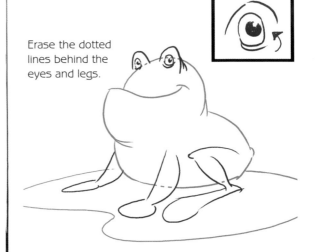

3

Erase the dotted lines around the feet and back.

4

Horse

1

2

The hard part is the legs. Take your time.

3

Draw hair shapes like the letter S.

Erase the dotted line that goes through the legs.

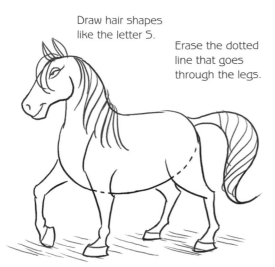

4

Dragon

1

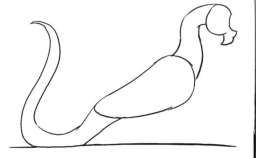

2

Erase the dotted lines by the tail, neck, and behind the legs.

3

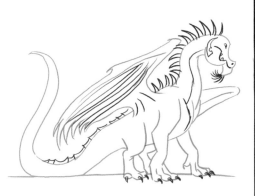

4

Jewelry

1

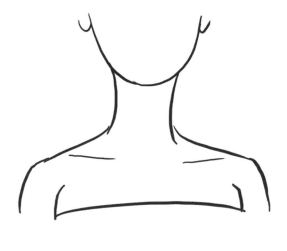

2

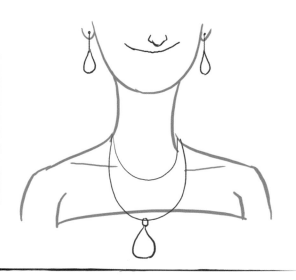

3

4

Bracelet

1

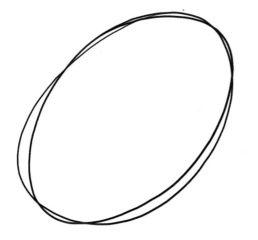

2

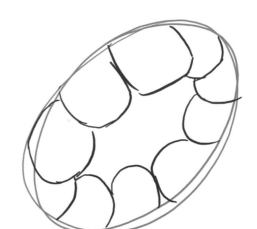

3

Erase the circles you drew in step 1.

4

Crown

1

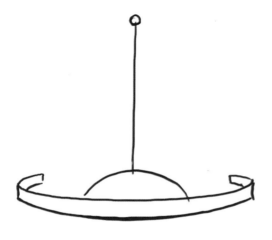

2

3

4

Tiara

1

2

3

4

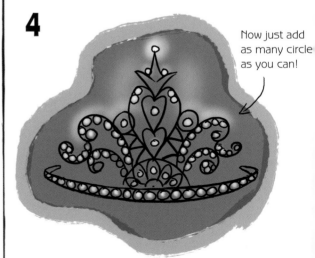

Now just add as many circle as you can!

Funky Shoe

1

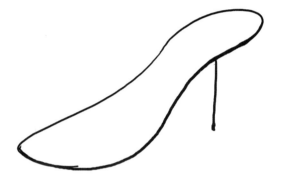

2

3

Erase the dotted lines underneath the big circle buckle.

4

Dancing Shoe

1

2

3

Erase the dotted lines that show through the straps.

4

Glass Slipper

1

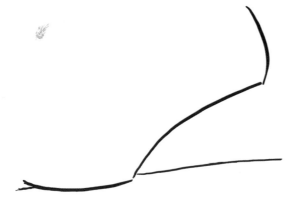

2

3

Add this line since we can see through the shoe.

4

Magic Wand

1

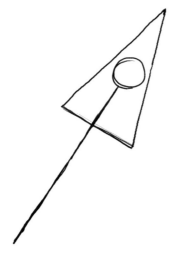

2

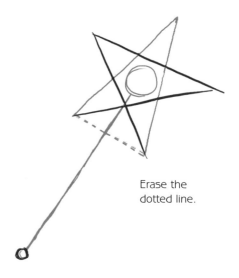

Erase the dotted line.

3

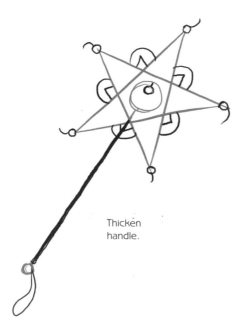

Thicken handle.

4

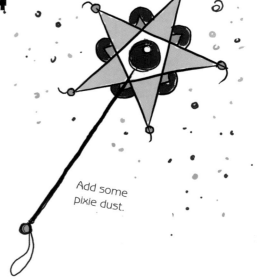

Add some pixie dust.

Pot of Gold

1

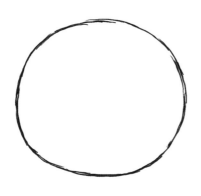

2

3

Erase the dotted line that shows through the rim.

4

Magic Mirror

1

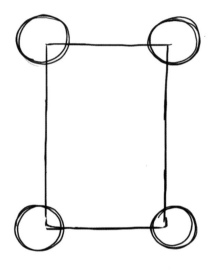

2

Erase the dotted lines at the corners.

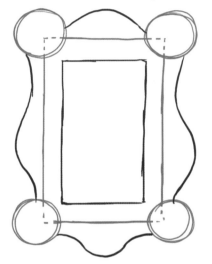

3

4

Throne

1

2

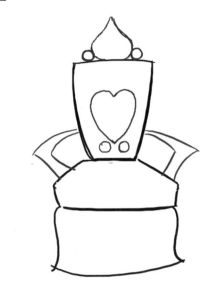

3

Erase the dotted lines inside the ends of the chair arms.

4

31

Bed

1

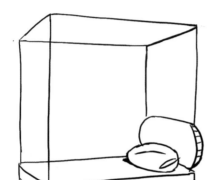

2

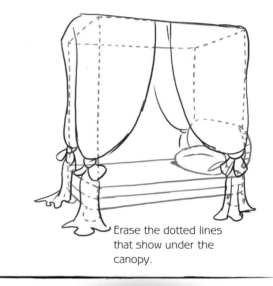

Erase the dotted lines
that show under the
canopy.

3

4

Tree

1

2

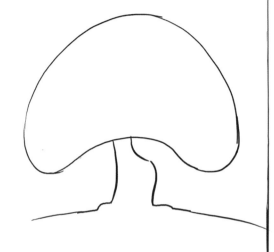

3

Erase the
dotted line
around the
treetop.

4

Carriage

1

Don't worry about making perfect circles.

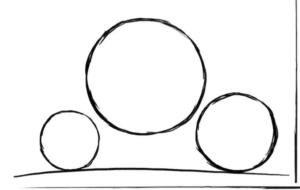

2

3

Erase the dotted lines that show through the wheel.

4

Castle

1

2

3

Erase the dotted lines
that show
under the balconies.

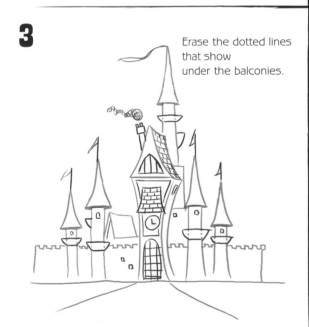

4

How to Write a Story

Write a Story in 5 Easy Steps

Are you ready to write a story to go with your drawings? Maybe you have a story you want to illustrate. Follow these five simple steps to make your very own story with drawings.

Step 1: Prewriting

Do you want to write about a princess or a prince? Maybe you have an idea for a story about a magic dragon. Keep in mind the drawings you want to use and base your story around them.

One way to begin your story is to answer these questions: Who? What? Why? Where? When? How?
For example:

Who is your princess?
What happens to her in your story?
Why is her story interesting?
Where and when does she live?
How does she react to her situation?

Here is a good brainstorming exercise: Fold a paper into six columns. Write the words *Who? What? Why? Where? When?* and *How?* at the top of each column. Write down every answer that comes into your head in the matching column. Do this for about five or ten minutes. Take a look at your list and pick out the ideas that you like the best. Now you are ready to write your story.

Princess Story Starters:

In a world where there aren't any . . .

The princess and her horse went to . . .

I knew that something very special
was about to happen . . .

The princess was sad because . . .

The king and queen knew that . . .

When the dragon woke from its
long sleep . . .

The people from a distant kingdom . . .

The day the prince came to town . . .

The princess needed a dress for . . .

Many years ago in a small village . . .

The princess met the evil witch . . .

In a magical kingdom called . . .

Step 2: Writing

Use the ideas from the list you made in Step 1. Write your story all the way through. Don't stop to make changes. You can always make changes later.

A story about a princess sitting on a rock isn't very interesting. What if the rock turns out to be a magic rock? What if the rock leads the princess to a secret kingdom? Your story will be more exciting if you don't make things too easy for the princess.

Step 3: Editing

Read your story. Is there a way to make it better? Rewrite the parts that you can improve. You might want to ask a friend or teacher to help. Ask them for their ideas.

Step 4: Proofreading

Make sure the spelling, punctuation, and grammar are correct.

Storyboarding

Check to see that your story works with your drawings. Find a table or other flat surface. Spread your drawings out in the order that goes with your story. Then place the matching text below each drawing. When you have your story the way you like it, go to Step 5. You can pick a way to publish your story.

Step 5:

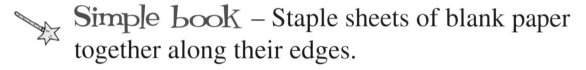

Publishing Your Book

You can make your story into a book.
There are many different forms your book
can take. Here are a few ideas:

Simple book – Staple sheets of blank paper
together along their edges.

Folded book – Fold sheets of blank paper in
half, then staple on the fold.

Hardcover book – Buy a blank hardcover
book. Then write your finished story in the book,
leaving spaces to add your art.

Bound book – Punch a few holes along the
edges of some pieces of paper. Tie them up or
fill the holes with paper fasteners. There are
many fun and colorful binding options at office
supply stores.

Digital book – Create a digital book using your computer. There are some great programs available. Ask an adult to help you find one that is right for you.

Our Story

You have finished the five steps of writing and illustrating a story. We bet you created a great story! Want to see ours? Turn the page and take a peek.

Princess Stella's Surprise

Princess Stella loved to ride her horse. Every day she would ride further and further away from her castle. One day she rode all the way to a stream on the edge of the castle's grounds. Stella and her horse stopped for a drink.

"That was refreshing!" the horse said.

"Neigh!" Stella replied. She tried again. All that came out was a whinny! A goose waddled up to Stella. "Princess, did you drink from the stream?" the goose asked. Stella nodded.

"An evil witch put a spell on this stream! Humans who drink from it talk like animals. Animals that drink from it talk like humans," the goose explained.

"Neigh, neigh," Stella said. She started to cry.

A frog jumped up next to her. "Don't cry, princess!" he said. "We'll help you!" The frog and the goose went into the stream. They came back pulling a magic mirror.

"Look into the mirror. You will see your fairy godmother," the goose said. Stella looked in the mirror. A beautiful woman appeared.

"Hello, Stella," the woman said. "I am your fairy godmother."

Stella tried to smile. "Neigh," she said. The fairy godmother gasped. "Oh no! You must have drunk from the stream!" Stella nodded.

"Look in your pocket, dear. You will find something that will help you." The fairy godmother disappeared. Stella reached into her pocket. She pulled out a magic wand! Stella began to wave the wand.

"H…Hello?" she said. The animals cheered. Stella turned her wand at the animals. "Please, don't!" the horse begged. "We want to talk!" Stella put the wand away. Every day after that, she and her horse went to the stream to chat with the goose and the frog. They were the best of friends forever after.

Further Reading

Books

Andrews, Julie, and Emma Walton Hamilton. The Very Fairy Princess. New York: Little, Brown Books for Little Readers, 2010.

Cech, John. The Princess and the Pea. New York: Sterling, 2007.

Lechermeier, Philippe. The Secret Lives of Princesses. New York: Sterling, 2010.

Levy, Barbara Soloff. How to Draw Princesses and Other Fairy Tale Pictures. Mineola, N.Y.: Dover Publications, 2008.

Watt, Fiona. How to Draw Princesses and Ballerinas. London: Usborne, 2005.

Internet Addresses

PBS Kids. Dot's Story Factory.
<http://pbskids.org/storyfactory/story.html>

Scholastic.com. Writing Games.
<http:// www.scholastic.com/kids/stacks/games/>

Index

A

animals, 15

B

bracelet, 22
brainstorming, 37
bed, 32

C

carriage, 34
castle, 35
crown, 23

D

dancing shoe, 26
dragon, 20

E

editing, 41

F

fairy godmother, 12

frogfish, 17
funky shoe, 25

G

glass slipper, 27
goose, 15

H

horse, 19

J

jewelry, 21

M

magic mirror, 30
magic wand, 28
mouse, 16

P

pot of gold, 29
prewriting, 36
prince, 11

princesses,
Drew, 8
Eva, 6
Trina, 7
Sierra, 9
Stella, 10
proofreading, 41
publishing, 42

S

story starters, 39
storyboarding, 41

T

tiara, 24
throne, 31
toad, 18
topic, 36
tree, 33

W

witch, 14
woodsman, 13
writing, 40